FRESH FRUIT DISHES

OVEN TEMPERATURES

F	C	GAS	TYPE
150°	70°	Lowest	cold
175°	80°	Lowest	cold
200°	100°	Lowest +	cold +
225°	110°	¼	very cool
250°	130°	½	
275°	140°	1	cool
300°	150°	2	
325°	170°	3	very moderate
350°	180°	4	moderate
375°	190°	5	moderate to
400°	200°	6	moderately hot
425°	220°	7	hot
450°	230°	8	
475°	240°	9	very hot
500°	250°	–	
525°	250°	–	
550°	290°	–	

METRIC CONVERSION

WEIGHT

1 Ounce   25 grams
2 Ounce   50 grams
3 Ounce   75 grams
4 Ounce   100 grams
5 Ounce   125 grams
6 Ounce   150 grams
7 Ounce   175 grams
8 Ounce   200 grams
½ Pound—200-250 grams.

1 Pound—500 grams.

VOLUME

⅛ Pint   60 Millilitre
¼ Pint   125 Millilitre
½ Pint   250 Millilitre
¾ Pint   375 Millilitre
1 Pint   500 Millilitre

1 ounce—25 grams as advised by The Metrication Working Party of the United Kingdom Federation for Education in Home Economics.

FRESH FRUIT DISHES

by

MARION HARRIS

BARRIE & JENKINS

COMMUNICA-EUROPA

This edition published in 1977
by Barrie & Jenkins Ltd
24 Highbury Crescent
London N5 1RX

ISBN 0 214 20318 2

Printed by Thomson Litho Ltd, East Kilbride,
Scotland

CONTENTS

INTRODUCTION

FRUIT is the most delicious form of natural food known to mankind and one of the essentials of a balanced diet. Not only does it play an important part in the digestion of other foods but it helps to strengthen the nerves. Without the special acid found in such fruits as peaches, apricots, apples, cherries and nectarines, headaches and biliousness may arise. Grapes are an excellent source of natural sugar; because they are easily digested they are particularly suitable for invalids.

While not rich in vitamins, grapes contain mineral salts which are especially effective in detoxifying the blood stream and cleansing the tissues. The combination of sodium, potassium, calcium and phosphorus, the mineral elements grapes are particularly rich in, has many other important functions to perform in the human organism. These minerals are absent in many of the foods which make up our daily diet.

All fruits, citrus fruits in particular, have a high vitamin content so essential to health and to fight infection. When buying oranges and lemons it is sometimes useful to have a little background knowledge so that you get real value for your money. Many South African oranges, for example, tend to be slightly greener than most. But this is by no means a sign that they are unripe or of poor quality. It merely indicates that they have been grown in a sub-tropical climate, where there is little change between night and day temperatures.

Another important point is the markings or small scars on some oranges at certain times of the season. This has no effect on the internal quality of the fruit. The marks are often caused by adjoining leaves or twigs.

This is equally true of lemons. Bruises and blemishes are no sign of inferior quality; but a green lemon should be avoided as this will defi-nitely be unripe.

Lemons bring out the flavour of other foods. For extra taste and freshness add a thin sliver of the yellow peel to stewing fruit. Add a dessertspoon of freshly squeezed juice to cold stewed prunes, apricots, peaches, apple-sauce and any fruit that has been cooked in heavy syrup. Add the juice of half a lemon to glasses of fruit squash, not only for the extra flavour but also for the Vitamin C that is so necessary to healthy teeth and skin.

One of the most nutritive of all fruits is the banana. Although imported while still unripe and green they are not usually sold until they are ready to eat. Once they are ripe they will turn black if kept longer.

Every average sized banana supplies you with 100 easily digested calories for fuel and energy, and in addition gives you a well rounded supply of vitamins and essential minerals. The banana is low in sodium, which makes it good for those on a reduced salt diet, and contains useful amounts of such necessary minerals as potassium, calcium, magnesium, copper, iron, phosphorous, sulphur, chlorine and iodine. Besides vitamins A and C, it has an excellent and available store of the B vitamins—thiamin, riboflavin and niacin. It even contains an appreciable amount of protein.

Not many fruits can be kept unless they are bottled or preserved. Citrus fruits and melons can be stored for a short period of time; lemons and limes, however, should be kept in a jar, covered with water. Medlars can be stored in wet bran.

Quinces should be laid out on shelves in a cool room. They should be kept separate from other fruits as they are apt to impart an unpleasant flavour to them.

Plums, peaches and nectarines can be stored for quite some time if sound fruit is wrapped individually in soft paper and laid in a dry, airy place, not touching each other.

To judge if apricots, peaches and red plums are ripe for good eating, go by the colour. Look at apricots and peaches all round the stalk end. A red flush on one side of the fruit means nothing. The skin round the stalk should have not the slightest tinge of green. When the green shade goes, the peach or apricot is ripe and ready for eating. It will be sweet, juicy and delicious.

Never judge the ripeness of a peach or apricot by squeezing—even after you have bought it, this fruit is very delicate and even a light squeeze will bruise and soften the flesh. Remove fruit from bag and place singly on dish so that no piece of fruit rests on another. It is really quite a good idea to keep the peaches in their loose paper wrappings up to the time when they are ready to serve.

Apples, too, should not touch each other when stored. Choice dessert apples should be wrapped in tissue paper or waxed paper.

Special trays are available for storing apples and pears. They can be picked straight into these trays and taken direct to the storeroom. When planning a storeroom for fruit choose a room which is cool but frost proof. It should be free from draught, though well ventilated, and slightly moist.

The fruit should be examined regularly and at the slightest sign of decay the damaged fruit should be removed otherwise the rest may be affected.

Before serving or displaying dessert pears and apples they should be rinsed in clean water, carefully dried and then polished with soft paper, or a soft clean cloth, to obtain a shine.

When fully ripe tomatoes are called for in a recipe, the expert shopper should look for all-over even redness. A fully ripe tomato is not only red all over the outside, it is also red all through. Seeds will be pinky (not green) and there will be little or no hard white fibre visible when the tomato is cut.

How do you know when a tomato is really fresh? The most delicate test is that of smell. A fresh tomato has an indescribable perfume unlike that of any other fruit or vegetable. It is faintly acrid, musky and fresh. Visible sign of freshness is the calyx. On a fresh tomato, these bits of grey-green leaves are still attached, still fresh looking as on a growing tomato. The longer the tomato is off the plant the more the calyx shrivels and dries. Finally it falls off, a sure sign that the tomato is no longer really fresh. If however, a few tomatoes in a whole pile are without the calyx do not assume lack of freshness. An occasional calyx will have been shaken off in the course of packing, despatch and quick handling in the shop.

I

HARD FRUITS

Apple Pie

Ingredients: 1½ lbs. cooking apples, 1 oz. sugar, 2 ozs. butter, 10 ozs. short crust pastry.

Divide the pastry in two. Roll out one half and line a tart tin with it. Peel, core and thinly slice the apples and cover the pastry with them. Sprinkle on the sugar and dot with butter. Roll out the remaining pastry and cover the apples with it. Prick the top pastry with a fork and brush with milk or beaten egg. Cook in a hot oven for 10 minutes, reduce the heat and cook more slowly for another 35 minutes.

Apple Charlotte

Ingredients: 1½ lbs. apples, 8 ozs. sugar, rind and juice ½ lemon, 2 ozs. butter, 2 tablespoons apricot jam, ¼ teaspoon cinnamon, 6 ozs. puff pastry.

Peel and core the apples and chop fairly small. Cook in a saucepan with the sugar, butter, jam, lemon rind and juice. Cook slowly and stir constantly until the apples are soft.

12

Line a pie dish with the puff pastry. Pour in the apple mixture and bake in a moderate oven for 50 minutes.

Serve with cream or custard sauce.

Apple Dumplings

Ingredients: 4 large cooking apples, 10 ozs. short crust pastry, 2 ozs. butter, 1 teaspoon cinnamon.

Divide the pastry into four and roll out each piece. Peel and core the apples. Mix together the butter, sugar and cinnamon and divide between the apples, filling the hole in the centre of each apple with it.

Stand the apples in the pastry and gather it up all round so that the apple is completely covered. Seal tightly. Steam for 45 minutes or bake in a moderate oven for 30 minutes.

Serve with cream or custard sauce.

Apple Turnover

Ingredients: 4 large cooking apples, 10 ozs. short crust pastry, 3 ozs. sugar, 1 oz. butter.

Roll out the pastry, not too thinly, and cut into rounds about 4 inches across.

Peel, core and chop the apples and cook with the sugar in a little water until they are soft, but not pulpy.

Place the apple mixture on one half of the pastry and fold the other half over. Crimp the edges together, prick on top and bake in a hot oven for 20 minutes.

Serve hot or cold.

Compôte Apples and Pears

Ingredients: 1 lb. cooking apples, 1 lb. cooking pears, 12 ozs. sugar, ¼ pint water, juice and peel 1 lemon, ½ lb. cherry jam.

Make a syrup by boiling together the sugar and water until it thickens. Peel, halve and core the apples and pears and cook them in this syrup a few at a time being careful to keep them unbroken. As each is cooked remove from syrup and arrange on serving dish filling the centre of each with jam.

After all have been cooked reboil the syrup adding the cores taken from the fruit and the orange juice and orange peel. Cook for about 15 minutes; test to see if a little will set on a cold plate. When ready strain the syrup over the fruit and leave to set. Serve with whipped cream.

Swedish Apple Cake

Ingredients: 8 ozs. biscuit crumbs or cake crumbs, 1½ lb. apples, peeled and sliced, 1 strip lemon peel, 1 oz. butter, ¼ lb. sugar.

Stew the apples with the lemon peel, sugar and a little water until very soft. Beat to a pulp. Fry the crumbs in the butter until slightly brown. Arrange alternate layers of crumbs and apple purée in a greased pie dish. Bake in a moderate oven for 30 minutes. Cool and turn out. Serve with vanilla sauce or whipped cream.

Scandinavian Bonde Pige

Prepare as above but substitute 4 ozs. brown breadcrumbs mixed with 2 ozs. of sugar in place of the cake or biscuit crumbs.

Apple Snow

Ingredients: 1½ lbs. apples, 1 egg white, 4 ozs. sugar, 1 teaspoon cinnamon.

Core and quarter the apples and stew in a little water. Drain and rub through a sieve, add half the cinnamon and 3 ozs. sugar. Beat the egg white until stiff and fold in the remaining sugar. Beat all together until the mixture is like snow. Pile high in a dish and garnish with the remainder of the cinnamon. Serve very cold with sponge fingers.

Apple Omelette

Ingredients: 2 large cooking apples, 4 well-beaten eggs, ½ oz. butter, caster sugar.

Peel and dice the apples and add them to the egg mixture. Place a little knob of butter in the heated omelette pan and pour $\frac{1}{4}$ mixture into the pan. After browning well serve at once with a good sprinkling of caster sugar. A sauce of warmed strawberry jam can be an optional extra.

Date and Apple Roll

Ingredients: 1½ lb. cooking apples, 4 ozs. chopped dates, 3 ozs. caster sugar, 3—4 tablespoons water, 8 ozs. short crust pastry.

Peel and slice the apples and bring to the boil with dates, sugar and water. Cook until tender. Allow to cool. Roll out pastry thinly and spread the mixture over it, leaving 1 in. all round. Brush edge with water. Roll up. Place on baking sheet with join underneath. Bake on middle shelf of oven at (360° F.) for 35—40 minutes. Serve with custard sauce.

Apple Purée Soup

Ingredients: 2 cups apple purée, 1 pint vegetable stock, 1 pint of water, 1 oz. sugar, 1 dessertspoon honey, 1 teaspoon cinnamon, 1 tablespoon cornflour, 1 egg, well beaten.

Blend the cornflour with a little of the cold water, Mix in the rest of the water, the vegetable stock and apple purée. Add the sugar and honey and simmer until the soup thickens. Stir in the beaten egg just before serving and sprinkle on the cinnamon.

Baked Apples Stuffed with Liver

Ingredients: 4 ozs. liver, 2 ozs. pork, 2 large cooking apples, wineglass of white wine, butter.

Wash the apples and remove core. Scoop out some of the apple and mince this together with the liver, pork, thyme and marjoram. Stuff the apple with this mixture and arrange them in a dish which has been greased with the butter. Add the wine. Cover and bake for 20 minutes in a moderate oven.

Apple and Macaroni Pudding

Ingredients: 4 ozs. macaroni, 1 lb. cooking apples, grated peel of lemon or orange, 1 egg white, 2 ozs. sugar, 2 tablespoons cream, breadcrumbs.

Cook the macaroni in boiling water. Drain as soon as it is tender. Line a well greased basin with the macaroni and sprinkle it with breadcrumbs.

Peel and core the apples and slice finely. Add the grated lemon or orange peel and fold in the egg white stiffly whisked, and the cream and sugar. Pile this mixture into the basin. Top with more breadcrumbs then a layer of macaroni. Dot the macaroni with butter, cover with a plate and bake in a moderately hot oven for about 1 hour.

Serve with custard sauce or a sweet white sauce.

Apple Crumble

Ingredients: 1½ lb. cooking apples, 4 ozs. margarine, 4 ozs. sugar, 4 ozs. flour, 2 ozs. desiccated coconut, a little water.

Peel, core and cut the apples into a greased pie dish. Mix together the margarine, sugar and flour until the mixture is like breadcrumbs. Pile on top of the apples, press into a mound, sprinkle the coconut over. Bake in a moderate oven for 40 minutes. Serve with cream or custard sauce.

Apple Fool

Ingredients: 2 lbs. cooking apples, 2 egg whites, 4 ozs. sugar, 4 ripe plums.

Peel and core the apples. Cook with a little water until tender. Rub through a sieve. Beat the egg whites until very stiff. Fold in the sugar, gradually add the apple purée. Arrange in individual dishes and garnish with the plums which have been halved and stoned. Chill before serving.

Note.—If plums are not available any other ripe fruit can be used to garnish.

Apple Rings in Butter

Ingredients: 4 large cooking apples, 3 ozs. butter.

Wash and core the apples but do not peel. Cut in slices about ½-inch thick.

Melt the butter in heavy frying-pan and fry the rings in it until they are crisp on the outside and soft inside. Drain well. Serve with cream.

Hot 'n' Cold Pears

Ingredients: For each person—1 chilled, sweet unpeeled dessert pear, 1 cup warm honey, lime juice or fresh lemon juice.

The pear should be chilled in the refrigerator or held under the cold tap for five minutes. Immediately before serving peel and core and lay, cut side downwards, in a shallow dish. Pour the warm honey and a little lemon or lime juice over the pear. Serve at once.

As an alternative to honey, hot chocolate sauce or custard sauce can be poured over the chilled pear.

Pear Beignets

Ingredients: 4 pears, 1 egg white, 1 well-beaten egg yolk, 1 cup flour, pinch salt, a little water, fresh lemon juice.

Make a fairly thick batter with the flour, salt, egg yolk and water. Slice the pears thickly and sprinkle with lemon juice. Add the egg white, stiffly beaten, to the batter and dip the pear slices into it. Make sure they are well covered then fry them in deep hot fat.

Pear and Ginger Fool

Ingredients: 1 lb. pears, 4 oz. sugar, 2 oz. finely-chopped preserved or crystallised ginger, 1 pint lemon custard.

Stew the pears and sugar in a little water until they are quite soft. Mash them and mix with the ginger, reserving a few pieces of the ginger to garnish. Mix with the lemon custard and pile in individual glasses. Top with pieces of ginger. Chill and serve.

Cheese and Pear Salad

Ingredients: For each serving—1 pear, 1 small lettuce, 2 dessertspoons salad oil, 1 heaped dessertspoon grated cheese, 1 dessertspoon fresh lemon juice, salt, pepper, paprika.

Roughly chop the pear and mix with the grated cheese. Make a dressing from the lemon juice, salad oil, salt, pepper and paprika. Toss the lettuce leaves in this until well coated. Arrange on a plate with the pear and serve immediately.

Spiced Stuffed Pear

Ingredients: For each serving—1 large, or 2
small pears, 2 oz. cottage cheese, 1 cup sugar, ¼
teaspoon cinnamon, glacé cherries, ' top-of-the-
milk '.

Peel and halve the pears. Remove the core.
Scoop out a little of the flesh and mash this
with the cottage cheese and ' top-of-the-milk '.
Mix sugar and cinnamon and roll the pears in it.
Stuff each half with the cheese mixture, sprinkle
any of the sugar and cinnamon that is left over
the top. Decorate with glacé cherries. Serve
with brown bread and butter.

Compôte of Pears

Ingredients: 1½ lb. cooking pears, ½ lb. cherry
jam, juice and rind of 1 orange, ¾ pint water,
¼ lb. sugar.

Boil the sugar and water together fast for
about 15 minutes until it starts to thicken. Peel,
halve and core the pears and cook them in this
syrup, a few at a time, taking care to keep them
unbroken. When cooked remove from syrup
and arrange on a serving dish. Fill the core
hollow with jam. When all the halves have been
cooked reboil the syrup, adding the orange peel
and juice and half the pear peelings and cores.
Cook for about 15 minutes until it will set

when tested on a cold plate. Strain over the fruit and leave until cold.

Serve with whipped cream.

Pear and Ginger Dumplings

Ingredients: 8 oz. plain flour, pinch salt, 4 oz. cooking fat, 2 tablespoons water, 4 medium cooking pears, 4 teaspoons Demerara sugar, 2 oz. chopped crystallised ginger.

Sieve the flour and salt and rub in the fat until the mixture resembles breadcrumbs. Add the water and mix to a dough. Divide into four.

Peel the pears and core, work from the bottom so that the top is left complete. Put 1 teaspoon Demerara sugar and quarter of the chopped ginger in each pear. Roll out each of the pieces of pastry. Cover the pears with pastry bringing the folds to the bottom. Place in a fireproof dish, brush with milk, sprinkle with sugar. Bake in fairly hot oven (400° F.) for 35—40 minutes.

Serve with custard.

Pear and Bramble Pudding

Ingredients: 1 lb. cooking pears, water to cover, 4 oz. sugar, 2 oz. self-raising flour, 2 oz. margarine, 1 egg, 2 heaped tablespoons bramble jelly.

Wash, peel and cut pears lengthways in quarters. Boil gently with water and 2 oz. sugar until pears are soft and the liquid is syrupy. Stir in bramble jelly. When dissolved remove from heat. Pour into medium-sized fireproof dish and leave to cool.

Sieve flour. Cream margarine with remaining sugar until light and fluffy. Beat in egg, adding a little of the sieved flour. When thick and creamy fold in the remaining flour. Grease the top of the fireproof dish, pile in the topping, spreading evenly and right to the sides. Bake in moderate oven (360° F.) for 35 minutes. Serve hot or cold.

Pear and Ham Rolls

Ingredients: 1 fresh lettuce, 1 lb. ripe pears, 6 large thin slices of boiled ham.

Peel and core the pears and chop fairly small. Line a serving dish or individual plates with lettuce leaves. Pile chopped pear onto each slice of ham and roll up. Arrange on lettuce and serve at once.

Spiced Pear Toast

Ingredients: 4 thick slices white bread, 2 ripe pears, 2 oz. sugar, 1 teaspoon cinnamon, butter.

Toast the bread on both sides. Spread one side at once with plenty of butter. Mix together sugar and cinnamon and sprinkle liberally over the buttered toast. Return to grill until sugar forms a slight crust. Serve at once on heated plates with thick slices of juicy freshly-cut pears on top.

II

STONE FRUITS

Cherry Strudel

Ingredients: ½ lb. plain flour, 2 oz. lard, salt, cherries, semolina.

Sift the flour and mix with 1 oz. lard. Make a well in the middle of the flour and pour in half a cup of warm water and a pinch of salt. Mix into a dough and knead thoroughly until the dough is smooth. Spread dough into a round shape, press with a rolling-pin, and then leave for thirty minutes.

Melt the remaining 1 oz. lard and pour a little of it over the dough. Place the dough onto a well-floured clean cloth. Stretch and spread the dough in all directions until it is quite thin. Now fold four times and sprinkle again with the hot lard. Place the sweetened, stoned cherries on it, sprinkle with semolina, and then roll up. Bake for about half an hour in a moderately hot oven (375° F. Reg. 4 or 5).

Cherry Dumplings

Ingredients: ½ lb. flour, ½ lb. Morella cherries, 1½ oz. butter, 2 egg yolks, 1 gill milk, 2 oz. breadcrumbs, 2 oz. melted butter, 2 oz. caster sugar.

Cream the butter, add the egg yolks, milk and breadcrumbs and mix to a smooth paste. Beat in the flour and a pinch of salt. Shape the dough into small dumplings with 2 cherries in the middle of each. Cook in boiling water for 5 minutes. Drain and arrange in serving dish with melted butter and sugar on top.

Cherry Sponge

Ingredients: 1 lb. stewed cherries, 4 oz. self-raising flour, 4 oz. margarine, 4 oz. caster sugar, 2 eggs, few drops almond essence, blanched and shredded almonds.

Well grease a 2-pint pie dish and place the stewed cherries in the bottom of it. Cream together the margarine and sugar until light and fluffy. Add the eggs, one at a time, beating thoroughly. Beat in the essence. Sieve the flour and then fold in with a metal spoon and spread the mixture over the cherries. Sprinkle with shredded almonds. Bake in a moderate oven (360° F. or Regulo 4) for 1—1¼ hours until it is well risen and golden.

Cherrie Pie

Ingredients: 8 oz. flour, 4 oz. lard, teaspoon salt, cold water to mix. Cherry filling: 3 cups fresh stoned cherries, ½ cup cherry juice, 1½ oz. cornflour, 1 cup sugar, 1 oz. butter or margarine, pinch salt, few drops almond essence.

To make pastry, sift together flour and salt, cut or rub in lard. Sprinkle with water, mixing lightly until dough forms. Turn onto floured pastry cloth and press dough together. Cover with waxed paper and leave to stand while preparing the filling.

Cherry Filling: Stew cherries in about 1 cup water. Drain. Combine cornflour and sugar and mix well, stir in the cherry juice and cook until thickened, stirring all the time. Add more sugar to taste. Stir in butter or margarine, salt and almond essence. Fold in cherries.

Divide dough in half. Roll out one half and line 9-inch greased baking plate. Fill with cherry mixture. Roll out remaining pastry to form cover. Bake in hot oven (425° F. or Reg. 6) for approximately 40 minutes.

Cherry and Orange Chantilly

Ingredients: 1 pint milk, 3 heaped tablespoons semolina, pinch salt, 2 oz. caster sugar, 2 eggs separated, finely grated rind of orange, orange segments, stewed cherries.

Blend the semolina with a little cold milk. Heat remaining milk with salt, orange rind and sugar. Add the semolina, bring to the boil and cook for a minute or two stirring constantly. Remove from heat, allow to cool slightly then beat in egg yolk. Cook over low heat for a minute. Remove and fold in stiffly-whisked egg whites. Pour into rinsed mould and leave to set.

Unmould onto serving dish and decorate with the stewed cherries and segments of orange.

Baked Peaches

Ingredients: 6 medium sized peaches, 1 oz. butter, 2 tablespoons sugar, 4 macaroons, (crushed), 1 egg yolk.

Cut 4 peaches in halves. Remove the stones and scoop out a little of the pulp from each half. Remove all the pulp from the remaining two peaches and mash it with the pulp removed from the halves. Add sugar, macaroons, butter and egg yolk and mix well. Well butter a baking dish, fill peach halves with the mixture and place them in the dish. Bake in a moderate oven for an hour. Serve hot or cold.

Peach Creams

Ingredients: Large firm peaches, 3 oz. ground almonds, 2 oz. icing sugar, 1 oz. butter, grated rind ½ lemon, 1 tablespoon orange juice, 3—4 tablespoons sherry, sugar.

Skin the peaches, cut in half and stone. Mix together the ground almonds, icing sugar, butter, orange juice and lemon rind. Fill the peach halves with mixture, join in pairs. Arrange in a fireproof dish, pour sherry over them and dredge thickly with sugar. Bake 20—25 minutes in a moderate oven or until sugar forms a syrupy glaze. Serve cold with custard or cream.

Peach Imperial

Ingredients: ½ lb. rice, 2 tablespoonfuls preserved fruit, 2 pints milk, 8 peaches, whipped fresh cream, vanilla essence, redcurrant jelly, kirsch liqueur (optional).

Cook the rice in the milk. When cold flavour with the vanilla essence and add the chopped preserved fruits. Arrange in a glass serving dish and pour over the kirsch and two glasses of whipped fresh cream.

Cook the peaches whole and in their skins for about 10 minutes, making sure that the liquid is not too concentrated. Peel them and cut neatly in half and remove stones. Arrange the half peaches on the rice. Cover with redcurrant jelly. Decorate with glacé cherries, pistaches and whipped cream. Serve very cold with more redcurrant jelly if desired.

Peach and Cheese Salad

Ingredients: Crisp leaves of lettuce, peaches, chive-flavoured cottage cheese.

Arrange the lettuce on a large platter or on individual plates. Slice peaches in half and stone. Skin also if preferred. Pile the chive-flavoured cheese into the centres of each peach half and arrange on the lettuce.

Peach Sundae

Ingredients: Sliced fresh peaches, whipped fresh cream, glacé cherries, chopped nuts.

Arrange peach slices in individual serving glasses and cover with the whipped fresh cream which should be stiff enough to pile into a mound in the centre. Decorate with chopped nuts and top with half a glacé cherry.

Peach Whip

Ingredients: 4 ripe peaches (fresh or stewed), 2 stiffly beaten egg whites, 3 oz. caster sugar, 4 oz. cream, glacé cherries.

If fresh peaches are used, peel and stone them. Sieve the fruit. Add half the sugar to the beaten egg whites and beat well. Add the rest of the sugar and the peach pulp. Continue beating until soft and fluffy. Whip the cream and pile on top and decorate with the cherries.

Peach Melba

Ingredients: 4 ripe peaches, 8 oz. vanilla ice-cream, ¼ lb. raspberries, 2 oz. sugar.

Melt the sugar over a low heat, add the raspberries and bring to the boil stirring all the time. Simmer until the fruit is soft (about 4 minutes) continuing to stir all the time. Sieve and then cool the purée.

Peel and stone the peaches. Divide the ice-cream into four serving dishes, put two halves into each dish, and pour a quarter of the cold purée on each.

Stuffed Peaches

Ingredients: 4 large peaches, 2 oz. macaroons, ½ oz. butter, 1 tablespoon sugar, 1 small egg yolk.

Halve the peaches, remove the stones and a little of the fruit. Crush the macaroons and mix with them the fruit pulp, egg yolk, sugar and butter. Fill the centres of the peaches with this mixture. Well butter a fireproof dish and arrange the filled peach halves in it. Bake in a moderate oven for 30 minutes.

Peach Flan

Ingredients: 3 large ripe peaches, 1 round sponge layer cake, ¼ cup fresh orange juice, 2 level tablespoons arrowroot or cornflour, 2 level tablespoons sugar, whipped cream, chocolate vermicelli or chopped almonds to decorate.

Sprinkle cake with a little of the fresh sweetened orange juice to moisten. Plunge peaches into boiling water for a minute and then skin. Allow to cool. Mix the arrowroot or cornflour and sugar in the top of a double boiler and stir until thickened. Heat remainder of orange juice and add to cornflour mixture. Cut skinned peaches in quarters and remove the stones. Arrange the quarters around the top of the cake like the spokes of a wheel. Pour the orange mixture over. Decorate with a blob of whipped cream in the centre and sprinkle each peach with chocolate vermicelli or chopped almonds.

Plums on Buttered Bread

Ingredients: 2 doz. ripe plums, 4 large slices white bread, 2 oz. butter, 2 oz. brown sugar.

Butter the bread on one side only. Stone the plums and arrange six on each buttered slice. Press down well. Dab with remaining butter and sprinkle with sugar.

Arrange the slices flat in a buttered fireproof dish, plum side up, and cover with buttered paper. Bake in a moderate oven for 30 minutes when the plums should be cooked in a syrup and the bread golden crisp.

Plum and Orange Fool

Ingredients: 1 lb. cooking plums (washed and stoned), ½ lb. sugar, I juicy orange, 1½ oz. quick-cooking tapioca, ¾ pint boiling water.

Cook the stoned plums gently in a covered saucepan. Little or no water need be added. When the plums are soft add the sugar. Cook for another minute, until the sugar is melted and the plums rather pulpy. Stir all the time.

Boil the ¼ pint water in a saucepan and when boiling add the tapioca. Cook slowly for 15 minutes until tapioca is soft and transparent. Cool both prepared fruit and tapioca. Add juice and grated rind of the orange to the fruit. Stir gently.

Combine fruit and tapioca mixture and pour into individual dishes or glasses. Chill. Place half a section of fresh peeled orange on each dish before serving and top with whipped cream or top-of-the-milk.

Plum Cake

Ingredients: 8 oz. flour, 3 oz. sugar, 2 oz. butter, 2 teaspoons baking powder, 2 tablespoons milk, 1 lb. plums, cinnamon.

Sift the flour and baking powder together, rub in the butter lightly and mix in 2 oz. sugar. Add enough milk to form a stiff paste. Roll this out to ¼ in. thick and lay it on a well-greased Swiss Roll tin. Peel and slice or halve the plums (removing stones) and arrange them on top of the pastry. Sprinkle with sugar and cinnamon. Bake in a hot oven for 25 minutes.

Damson Crumble

Ingredients: 1½ lb. damsons (washed and stoned), 2 oz. margarine, 1 oz. flour, 2 oz. rolled oats, 1 teaspoon cinnamon, 4 oz. brown sugar, 3—4 tablespoons water.

Place the damsons in a greased, fireproof dish and sprinkle with half the sugar. Add water. Mix together the flour, oats, cinnamon and remaining sugar. Sprinkle this mixture on top of damsons and bake in a moderate oven (350° F.) for 30—40 minutes.

Damson Delight

Ingredients: 1 lb. damsons, 4 oz. brown sugar, 3 oz. flour, 3 oz. caster sugar, 3 oz. butter, 1 egg.

Stone and slice the damsons. Cream together the butter, and sugar and add the lightly beaten egg alternately with spoonfuls of the sieved flour.

Grease a pie dish, turn in half the mixture, sprinkle with some of the sugar and spread the sliced damsons on it. Quickly sprinkle with the rest of the sugar and cover with the remainder of the sponge mixture. Bake in a moderate oven until golden brown—about 40 minutes at 350° F.

Apricot Tart

Ingredients: 6 oz. prepared sweet pastry, 2 lbs. apricots, 2 oz. sugar, vanilla flavouring.

Cook the apricots in a little water with the sugar and a few drops of vanilla. Cut them in half and remove stones. Roll out the prepared pastry and cover a greased baking tin or sheet with it. Arrange the apricots on the pastry. Cook in a hot oven for 20 minutes. Reduce heat and cook for a further 10 minutes.

Apricot Cheese Salad

Ingredients: 1 lb. ripe apricots, ½ lb. cottage cheese, 2 oz. chopped peanuts, slices of preserved ginger, cress or lettuce.

Halve the apricots and remove the stones. Arrange on serving platter or individual plates surrounded by crisp lettuce or cress. Fill the apricot centres with cottage cheese piled into a mound. Top with a slice of ginger and sprinkle with chopped peanuts.

Plum Whip

Ingredients: ¾ lb. plums, ¼ pint water, 2 oz. sugar, 1 pint packet jelly, ½ pint hot water, vanilla ice-cream.

Stew the plums in the ¼ pint water with the sugar. Pass the plums through a sieve.

Make up the jelly (red or yellow for red plums, yellow or green for golden plums) in the ½ pint hot water. When dissolved mix with the plum purée in a measuring jug. Together they should make up 1 pint, if necessary a little more water can be added. When the mixture is almost set whisk vigorously and turn into individual serving glasses. Top with portions of ice-cream before serving.

Plum Splits

Ingredients: ½ lb. ripe dessert plums, 2 oz. sugar, vanilla ice-cream, chopped nuts.

Wash, split and stone the plums. Mix with the sugar and leave to stand for at least an hour. Divide the ice-cream into individual serving dishes and top with plums and syrup. Sprinkle the chopped nuts over.

Plum Pie

Ingredients: 1½ lb. plums; a little water, sugar to taste, 6 oz. self-raising flour, pinch salt, ¼ teaspoon grated nutmeg, 1 teaspoon ground cinnamon, 2 oz. caster sugar, 2 oz. margarine, ¼ pint milk, beaten egg.

Wash and remove stones from the plums and place in a pie dish with a little water and sugar to taste.

Sieve together flour, nutmeg, cinnamon and

2 oz. sugar. Cut and rub in the margarine, mix to a soft dough with the milk. Roll out to a thickness of ¾ in. Cut into strips ½ in. wide. Arrange these lattice-wise over the plums. Brush with beaten egg and cook at 450° F. for 10—15 minutes. Reduce heat to 350° F. and cook for a further 35 minutes. Serve hot or cold.

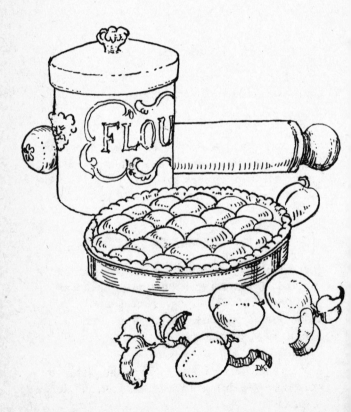

III

SMALL SOFT FRUIT

Blackcurrant and Apple Pie

Ingredients: 8 oz. prepared pastry, ½ lb. stewed apples, ¼ lb. blackcurrants, 2 oz. sugar, a little milk or white of egg.

Divide the pastry in two, line a tart tin with one half. Spread lightly with melted butter then arrange the stewed apples on it. Sprinkle the cleaned and prepared blackcurrants over the apples, sprinkle with the sugar. Roll out the remaining pastry and cover. Prick the top with a fork and brush with white of egg or milk. Bake in hot oven for 10 minutes, reduce heat and bake for another 35 minutes.

Blackcurrant and Apple Shortbread

Ingredients: 1 lb. fresh blackcurrants, ½ lb. sugar 1 oz. gelatine soaked in 3 tablespoons cold water, ½ pint thick custard, 2 medium sized apples, 12 wedge shaped pieces of shortbread.

Peel and cook the apples with a little of the sugar until they form a pulp. Beat well with fork, or sieve. Leave to cool.

Cook the blackcurrants with the remainder of
the sugar and just sufficient water to cover. Add
the gelatine to the hot purée, stir until dissolved, then set aside to cool. When just beginning to thicken pour half this mixture into a
9-in. pie plate which has been rinsed in cold
water. Allow to set. Whip together the custard
and apple sauce and spread over the blackcurrant purée. Chill. Top with remaining
blackcurrant jelly and chill again. Before serving decorate with piped fresh whipped cream
or butter cream. Top with the wedge-shaped
shortbread arranged to resemble cut portions
of pie crust.

Summer Pudding

Ingredients: Slices of white bread about ¼ in.
thick, 1 lb. black or red currants, 8 oz. sugar,
a little water.

Stew the currants with very little water and
the sugar to taste.

Fit a round of bread to the bottom of a pudding basin and line the sides of the basin with
fingers of bread. Fill up the basin with alternate
later of hot stewed fruit and slices of bread.
finishing with a round of bread on top.

Cover with a plate with a weight on it and
put to cool. Turn out and serve with cream or
custard sauce. It may be necessary to drain off
surplus liquid before turning the pudding out.

Red Currant and Raspberry Tart

Ingredients: 1 cooked flan or tart case, 1½ lbs. raspberries, ½ lb. red currants, 6 oz. caster sugar, 1 tablespoon red currant jelly.

Prepare the fruit, add the sugar and cook for 5 minutes, stirring gently all the time, so that the fruit remains whole. When the sugar has melted and formed a syrup, strain and put the fruit in the cooked case. Bake in a moderate oven for 10 minutes.

Add the red currant jelly to the juice and pour over the fruit when cool. Serve cold, with cream.

Whipped Raspberries

Ingredients: 1 lb. raspberries, 1 lb. sugar, 2 egg whites.

Bruise the fruit with a wooden spoon and add the sugar. Stir well. Beat the egg whites until stiff. Stir into the raspberry mixture and beat—using egg whisk—till everything is thoroughly mixed. Chill. Serve with cream.

Raspberry Meringue Pie

Ingredients: 1 cooked flan or tart case, ½ lb. raspberries, 2 tablespoons cornflour, 4 table-spoons sugar, 2 egg yolks, grated lemon rind, 2 egg whites, 4 oz. caster sugar, a little water.

Cook the raspberries with a little water until quite soft. Sieve to a purée and make up to $\frac{1}{2}$ pint with extra water if necessary.

Mix the cornflour to a thin paste with a little water then add the raspberry purée. Return to pan and cook till mixture thickens. Stir constantly to prevent lumps forming. Add 4 tablespoons sugar, egg yolks, and lemon rind and reheat gently to ensure egg is cooked. Cool, then transfer to the prepared flan case.

Whip the egg whites until stiff, add caster sugar little at a time until about half has been beaten in. Fold in the remainder. Pile the meringue around the edges of the flan and flash bake at 475° F. (Reg. 9) for 3 minutes or till meringue is golden. Serve hot or cold with whipped cream.

Raspberry Quencher

Ingredients: $\frac{1}{2}$ lb. ripe raspberries, $1\frac{1}{2}$ pints chilled milk, 2 tablespoons sugar, pinch salt, vanilla ice-cream.

Crush raspberries and combine with the milk. Pass through a sieve. Add pinch salt and sugar.

Spoon ice-cream into long glasses and pour in raspberry milk. If liked, top with whipped cream.

Raspberry Shortbread Trifle

Ingredients: $1\frac{1}{2}$ lb. raspberries, $\frac{1}{2}$ pint milk, 3 oz. sugar, 3 eggs, few drops almond essence, 12 shortbread biscuits, 3 tablespoons whipped cream, few pieces of angelica for garnish.

Gently stew the raspberries with 2 oz. sugar and very little water. Strain off the syrup and reserve it. Place the raspberries in a glass serving bowl. Warm the milk and 1 oz. sugar. Beat the eggs and stir into the milk. Cook over boiling water (double saucepan) until thick and creamy. Do not allow this custard to boil. Add the almond essence. Cool and pour over the raspberries. Dissolve the gelatine in ½ pint of the heated raspberry syrup. Chill and when just setting pour over the set custard. Chill again. Spike round the edges with the shortbread, reserving four pieces to decorate the top. Make a border with the whipped cream, and a centre blob. Decorate this and the shortbread with pieces of angelica.

Currant Creams

Ingredients: 1 lb. red or blackcurrants, 2 oz. sugar, ¼ pint water, 2 oz. cornflour, ½ pint double cream, crisp biscuits.

Prepare the currants and cook gently with the sugar and water until soft. Blend the cornflour with a little cold water and add to the currant mixture. Cook, stirring occasionally, for about 5 minutes. Leave until quite cold.

Lightly whip the cream and fold it into the currant mixture. Place into individual dishes and chill slightly. Serve with crisp biscuits.

Red Currant and Banana Flan

Ingredients: 1 lb. red currants, 3 bananas, ½ lb. sugar, 2 level dessertspoons arrowroot or cornflour, 1 short crust pastry case baked blind, a little whipped cream.

Prepare the currants and put in pan with almost ½ teacup water. Cook slowly, mashing fruit with the back of a wooden spoon. When fruit is soft drip through a jelly bag or rub through a fine hair sieve. Add sugar and make up to ¾ pint by adding water if necessary. Return to pan and heat until sugar has melted. Blend cornflour with a little water then add to mixture. Cook for a few minutes, stirring all the time until mixture is thick and clear. Allow to cool. Slice bananas into baked pastry case, spoon red currant mixture over and decorate with a border of piped whipped cream, or with a large blob of cream in centre.

Kisyeli

Ingredients: 1 lb. red currants, ½ lb. blackcurrants, ½ lb. raspberries, 2 oz. ground rice, 4 oz. sugar.

Stew the fruit with the sugar and just enough water to prevent the mixture sticking to the pan. Strain off the juice. Use a little to mix ground rice to a paste. Heat the remaining juice and stir into the ground rice. Return to pan and cook for 4—5 minutes, stirring all the time. Chill and serve with whipped cream.

Kaltschale

Ingredients: 1 lb. soft fruit (raspberries, strawberries, red or blackcurrants can be used), 5 oz. sugar, 1½ pints scalded and chilled milk.

Cook the berries until they are just tender. Pass them through a sieve. Whisk up this fruit purée with the sugar until it is frothy and light. Mix into it the milk. Place in refrigerator until very cold.

Blueberry Pie

Ingredients: 10 oz. short crust pastry, 1 lb. bilberries, 4 oz. sugar, 1 oz. butter, 1 oz. flour.

Line a greased flan tin with half the pastry. Wash the bilberries and dredge with flour. Arrange on the pastry, sprinkle with the sugar and dot with butter. Cover with remaining pastry, making a hole in the middle to allow steam to escape. Bake in hot oven for 30 minutes.

Blackberry Cream Flan

Ingredients: 1 7-in. prepared flan case, 1 lb. blackberries, 4 oz. brown sugar, 1 level dessertspoon custard powder, 2 oz. caster sugar, 4 oz. whipped cream, ½ pint milk.

Stew the blackberries with the brown sugar until tender (about 20 minutes). Use just enough water to cover fruit. Save some of the large berries for decoration and put the rest through a medium coarse sieve. Make up the custard powder with the milk and sugar (less one teaspoon) and stir in the sieved blackberry purée. Pour into the pastry shell and spread smooth. Whip the egg white very stiffly with the teaspoon of sugar and gradually fold into the whipped cream. Pipe on top of flan, and top each rosette with a blackberry.

Blackberry Pancakes

Ingredients: 1 cup blackberries, 1 cup flour, 1 cup milk, 2 oz. sugar, 1 egg, 2 oz. butter.

Mix the egg yolk and sugar together, beat in the sifted flour and the blackberries. Add 1 oz. melted butter and fold in the stiffly beaten egg white. Melt a little fat in a frying-pan, cook spoonfuls of the mixture on both sides.

Blackberry Fluff

Ingredients: 1 lb. blackberries, 4 oz. sugar, 3 egg whites, juice and rind of ½ lemon, 1 oz. gelatine.

Stew the blackberries, strip of lemon rind and sugar in a little water until tender. Pass through a sieve. Dissolve the gelatine in a little water, pour the fruit purée into it. Add the lemon juice and sufficient water to make up to 1 pint. Leave in a cold place. When almost set fold in the stiffly whisked egg whites.

Blackberry Roll

Ingredients: 8 oz. biscuit dough, $\frac{1}{2}$ lb. blackberries, 1 oz. butter, $\frac{1}{2}$ pint apple sauce, cinnamon, 1 oz. caster sugar.

Roll out biscuit dough to about $\frac{1}{2}$-in. thick. Melt butter and brush dough well with it. Strew the blackberries over dough and cover with caster sugar and dusting of cinnamon. Fold and roll the dough. Place on a greased dish, surround with blackberries and bake in moderate oven 30 minutes. Serve with apple sauce.

Blackberry Batter Pudding

Ingredients: $\frac{1}{2}$ lb. blackberries, 4 oz. flour, 2 oz. sugar, pinch salt, 1 egg, $\frac{1}{2}$ pint milk, $\frac{1}{2}$ oz. butter.

Beat together the egg, milk and sugar. Mix together the dry ingredients, make a well in the middle and gradually beat in the egg mixture. Leave to stand for 1 hour. Wash the blackberries. Heat the fat in a pie dish that measures approx. 8 in. x 12 in. and pour in the batter. Add the blackberries. Bake in a hot oven (400° F.) for 40 minutes.

Serve hot with custard sauce.

Grape Glory

Ingredients: 1 ready-made plain sponge, ½ lb. large grapes, 2 tablespoons jam desiccated coconut or chopped nuts to decorate, ¼ cup water, ¼ cup sugar, a little whipped cream.

Warm the jam and thin down with a little water. Spread a thin layer all over the sponge, including the sides. Sprinkle the sides with the desiccated coconut or nuts. Arrange the grapes on the top of the sponge.

Boil the sugar and water together for 5 minutes and allow to cool. Pour this syrup over the top of the grapes. Decorate with whipped cream.

Grape Purée

Ingredients: 1 lb. grapes, ½ pint cream, nuts to garnish.

Cook the grapes in a little water until soft, then pass them through a sieve. Leave to cool and then mix with cream. Serve in cups or glasses, decorate with nuts.

Grape Salad

Ingredients: ½ lb. black and white grapes, 8 ripe red apples, 1 small pineapple, glacé cherries, ¼ pint double cream, 3 oz. sugar, ¼ pint water.

Boil the sugar and water together until they thicken and form a syrup. Wash and dry the apples thoroughly. Cut a slice from the top of each and remove the inside very carefully. The skins should be unbroken and so should the bottom of the apple. Mix the apple pulp with shredded pineapple pulp, glacé cherries and the grapes which have been halved and seeded. Fill the apple cases with this mixture and arrange in serving dishes.

Pour sugar syrup over fruit to prevent it discolouring. Serve with whipped cream piped on top.

Grape Meringue Tart

Ingredients: 1 shortcrust pastry shell, 1 lb. white grapes, ½ lb. icing sugar, 4 tablespoons sherry, 3 egg whites, 4 oz. caster sugar.

Seed the grapes. Cover with icing sugar and wine and allow to stand. Beat egg whites until frothy. Add 2 oz. caster sugar and beat until stiff. Fold in remaining 2 oz. sugar. Pile meringue on pastry shell and bake in a slow oven until lightly coloured. Heap grapes over meringue just before serving.

Grape Glacé

Ingredients: ½ lb. black and white grapes, 4 pears, 2 dessert apples or 1 small melon, juice 1 orange, 3 tablespoons red currant jelly, ½ pint water, ½ teaspoon cornflour, 2 oz. butter.

Make a syrup by heating red currant jelly, water and orange juice together for a few minutes. Strain and add cornflour which has first been blended with a little cold water. Add butter and reheat. Stir until it begins to thicken. Peel, seed and cut melon into chunks, or peel, core and quarter apples. Peel, core and quarter pears. Put cut-up fruit in saucepan with half the syrup and cook very gently until they are fairly soft. Place in serving dish, pouring the hot syrup over them. Cut grapes in half and seed. Arrange these on top of the cooked fruit when it is quite cold. Pour over remaining syrup which has also been allowed to cool. This will glaze the grapes yet leave them fresh and crisp.

Serve with whipped cream or ice-cream.

IV

LARGE SOFT FRUIT

Gooseberry Fruit Fool

Ingredients: 2 lb. green gooseberries, 6 oz. sugar, ½ pint cream.

Wash, top and tail the gooseberries, then cook in a little water until soft enough to mash. Add the sugar and beat well. Rub through a sieve then mix in the cream with the purée. Chill thoroughly before serving.

Gooseberry Shortbread

Ingredients: 1 lb. gooseberries, 6 oz. sugar, 3 tablespoons water, ¼ pint custard, whipped cream and glacé cherries to garnish, shortbread fingers.

Stew the gooseberries gently with the sugar and water. Rub through a sieve. When cool whisk with the custard. Sweeten further to taste if desired. Arrange in serving cups and top with a blob of whipped cream and half a glacé cherry. Serve with crisp shortbread fingers.

Gooseberry Crumble

Ingredients: 1 lb. gooseberries, 6 oz. caster

sugar, ¼ pint water. Topping—3 oz. plain flour, ¼ level teaspoon salt, 2 oz. cooking fat, 2 oz. rolled oats, 2 oz. caster sugar.

Top and tail and wash the gooseberries. Stew gently with the sugar and water until soft. Drain off the juice and keep for serving. Place the fruit in the bottom of an 8-in. fireproof dish.

To make the topping sieve the salt and flour into mixing bowl. Rub in the cooking fat until the mixture resembles breadcrumbs. Add the rolled oats and sugar. Sprinkle this mixture over the fruit. Bake in moderately hot oven for 35—40 minutes, until the crumble is crisp. Serve with the fruit juice.

Strawberry Yoghourt

Ingredients: 12 oz. plain yoghourt, ¼ pint chilled milk, 3 tablespoons orange juice, 4 tablespoons sliced fresh strawberries.

Mix all the ingredients together and whisk until smooth and frothy. Sweeten to taste if necessary.

Strawberry Snow

Ingredients: 1 packet strawberry jelly, 1 pint boiling water, 1 egg white, 1 tablespoon caster sugar, ¼ pint fresh whipped cream, ½ lb. strawberries.

Dissolve the jelly in the boiling water. When

cold and beginning to set whisk in the egg white and sugar which have previously been whipped to a stiff snow. Whisk in the cream. Reserve a few of the berries for decoration, slice the remainder and fold into the mixture. Turn into individual dishes and garnish with the whole berries.

Strawberry Mould

Ingredients: 16 triangles of shortbread, 1 packet strawberry jelly cream, 1 pint milk, ½ lb. fresh strawberries, cream to decorate.

Heat the milk and pour over jelly crystals. Mix until they are well dissolved. When cool pour into a lightly oiled border mould. Leave to set.

Line a circular dish with the shortbread. When jelly cream has set carefully turn it out onto this shortbread-lined dish. Fill the centre with strawberries, piling them high. Decorate the edges of the border shape with rosettes of cream.

Serve with extra cream and sugar.

Strawberry Ice-cream

Ingredients: 1 lb. strawberries, ½ pint cream, 4 egg yolks, ¼ lb. caster sugar.

Beat the egg yolks and put into a double

saucepan with the cream. Cook very slowly, stirring until it thickens. Add the sugar and the crushed strawberries.

Freeze in the ice tray of a refrigerator turned to its lowest temperature. Stir every half an hour.

Strawberry Shortcake

Ingredients: 1 lb. strawberries, ½ lb. flour, 2 eggs, 1½ oz. sugar, 1 oz. butter, 1 dessertspoon baking powder, milk, icing sugar.

Sieve together the flour and baking powder, add the sugar. Cut the butter into the mixture with a knife. Beat the eggs and stir them in. Mix with enough milk to bind. Roll out and place in a tart tin. Bake in a hot oven for 20 minutes. Remove from tin and arrange on serving plate. Slice in half and fill with the prepared strawberries. Large berries should be halved or, if necessary, quartered. Replace the cut half and sprinkle with icing sugar.

Strawberry Mousse

Ingredients: 1 lb. prepared strawberries, 12 oz. caster sugar, pinch salt, 1 pint thick cream, teaspoonful vanilla essence.

Mash fruit and sugar together, add pinch salt. Whip together the cream and vanilla essence. Fold in the mashed fruit and turn into mould. Place in freezing compartment of refrigerator. When frozen turn out and serve garnished with whole fruit.

Strawberry Sundae

Ingredients: Strawberries, whipped cream, nuts to decorate.

Crush the fruit and place in individual serving glasses. Top with whipped cream. Sprinkle with nuts.

Baked Bananas

Ingredients: 6 firm bananas, cream, 1 dessertspoonful lemon juice, 3 oz. Barbados sugar, 1¼ oz. butter, 3 tablespoons desiccated coconut.

Peel the bananas and arrange them in a fireproof dish, sprinkle the lemon juice over them and then cover with the brown sugar. Dot all over with small pieces of butter and sprinkle on the coconut.

Bake in a moderately hot oven for about 20 minutes, until the bananas are soft but not squashy. Just before serving pour the thick, cold cream over.

Banana Fritters

Ingredients: 4 bananas, 4 oz. plain flour, pinch salt, 1 egg, ¼ pint milk, caster sugar, cooking fat for deep frying (enough to make a 3-inch depth in pan).

Sieve the flour and salt into a basin. Make a well in the centre, add the egg and the milk gradually, mixing with the flour until the batter reaches a coating consistency. Peel the bananas, cut in half lengthwise and cut each piece in half crosswise. Heat the cooking fat until it reaches 360° F. (To test without thermometer drop a one-inch cube of day-old bread into it; it should turn golden brown in 1 minute). Using a skewer to hold the pieces of banana, dip each one into the batter. Drain off surplus before lowering into hot fat. Cook 3 or 4 fritters at a time. Turn so that they are evenly browned on each side. Lift out with a slice or kitchen spoon that is perforated. Drain on crumpled kitchen paper. Sprinkle with caster sugar and serve immediately.

Banana Sundae

Ingredients: For each Sundae—1 ripe banana cut into 4 pieces, 1 heaped tablespoon vanilla ice-cream, 1 tablespoon strawberry syrup, 3 or 4 fresh strawberries, cherries or other berries, whipped cream.

Make the strawberry syrup by mixing equal quantities strawberry jam and water, beating well and stirring. Do not strain.

Place the ice-cream into an individual serving dish, arrange the 4 pieces of banana around it, pour the syrup over the ice-cream and top up with the whipped cream. Garnish with the fresh strawberries or other fruit, either whole or sliced.

Banana Split Salad

Ingredients: For each portion—1 banana, 1 dessertspoonful cottage cheese, 2 or 3 strawberries or chopped nuts, sprig of watercress.

Peel the banana and split it lengthwise. Pile the cottage cheese in the centre. Garnish with the watercress and sliced strawberries or nuts.

Banana Supreme

Ingredients: 1½ pints milk, 4 bananas, 3 oz. fine semolina, 3 tablespoons sherry, 3 egg whites, 6 oz. caster sugar.

Boil the semolina in the milk, sweeten to taste, stirring constantly. When smooth, but not too thick, add 2 tablespoons of the sherry. Pour into a deep buttered fireproof dish.

Peel the bananas and slice lengthwise and cover the semolina mixture with them. The surface should be completely covered. Sprinkle over the rest of the sherry. Make a meringue topping with the egg whites and caster sugar.

Pile this over the bananas. Bake in a slow oven
—Mark 1 or 250° F.—for 1 hour to crisp the
meringue.

Banana Chips

Ingredients: Bananas, deep fat for frying, salt,
cayenne pepper.

Peel the bananas and cut into very thin slices.
Fry quickly in deep fat until brown. Drain and
sprinkle with a little salt and cayenne pepper.

Banana Cream Flip

Ingredients: 2 bananas, 4 oz. creamed cottage
cheese, ½ pint milk, brown sugar to taste or
golden syrup.

Mash the bananas and beat in the cheese.
Gradually whisk in the ½ pint milk. Sweeten to
taste.

Creole Fried Bananas

Ingredients: 6 bananas, deep fat or oil, 4 tablespoons rum, 1 tablespoonful brown sugar, batter.

Peel the bananas and cut into 4 pieces. Place
in a shallow dish and sprinkle on the sugar.
Pour the rum over them. Leave for ½ hour,
turning occasionally.

Drain off surplus sugar and rum into the
batter. Mix thoroughly then dip each piece of

banana into the batter and fry in the boiling fat until light brown. Lift with slice or perforated spoon, drain well, sprinkle with sugar and serve.

Banana Trifle

Ingredients: 6 bananas, ½ pint cream, 4 tablespoons sherry, 2 tablespoons apricot jam, chopped nuts or a few glacé cherries.

Peel 5 of the bananas and cut them lengthwise. Spread with jam and pour over the sherry. Leave for 1 hour. When ready to serve, whip the cream for about five minutes, spread over and decorate with the remaining banana, peeled and cut in thin slices and the nuts or glacé cherries.

Creamed Bananas

Ingredients: 4 ripe bananas, 3 oz. caster sugar, ¼ pint sherry, ½ pint cream.

Peel the bananas, mash and sieve them. Add the sugar and mix well. Add the cream and whisk for 10 minutes or until thick. Gradually beat in the sherry. Well chill.

Banana Waldorf

Ingredients: 2 bananas, 3 apples, 1 head celery, ¼ lb. walnuts, mayonnaise, salt and pepper.

Peel and slice the bananas and apples, chop the celery and walnuts. Mix all together, season with salt and pepper. Serve mayonnaise separately.

Bananas au Rhum

Ingredients: 5 large bananas, 2 tablespoonfuls rum, 3 tablespoonfuls Demerara sugar, juice of 1 lemon, 3 tablespoonfuls water, ½ oz. butter, whipped cream.

Use the butter to well grease a shallow fireproof dish. Cut the bananas in half lengthwise and arrange in the dish. Sprinkle on the sugar and lemon juice and water. Bake in a moderate oven for 35 minutes or until brown. Just before cooking is completed add the rum.

Serve with whipped cream handed separately. A little rum may be whisked into the cream for additional flavour if desired.

Savoury Banana Spread

Ingredients: 2 large bananas, 1 breakfastcup minced, cooked lamb, veal or chicken, 1 oz. butter, 1 tablespoon mayonnaise, 1 dessertspoon fresh chopped parsley, juice and grated rind ½ lemon, salt and pepper to taste.

Cream butter, mix in meat and parsley. Slice and mash bananas and mix with mayonnaise and mix well with the meat mixture. Add seasoning and lemon juice last.

Serve on hot toast with celery as an optional extra.

Sweet Banana Spread

Ingredients: 3 or 4 bananas, 1 small tin evaporated milk, 1 dessertspoon strawberry jam, 2 teaspoons lemon juice, pinch salt.

Slice and beat the bananas, beat evaporated milk with salt until very thick, stir in the jam. Sprinkle lemon juice over bananas, stir into cream. Use as a filling for brown or white bread sandwiches, or as a spread on toast. No butter will be necessary.

Banana Rum Butter

Ingredients: 1 banana, 4 oz. butter, ½ lb. soft brown sugar, 2 tablespoons Dark Jamaica rum, grated nutmeg.

Cream butter and work in sugar using the back of a wooden spoon. Peel, slice and mash banana and mix in with butter and sugar. Add rum and light grating of nutmeg.

Serve as a sauce for hot steamed pudding or as a spread.

This spread can be kept if packed into a pot or jam jar and kept in a cold place. It may harden a little with keeping.

Banana Curry

Ingredients: 4 large firm bananas, 1 onion, 1 large apple, 4 oz. butter, 1 heaped dessertspoon flour, 2 teaspoons curry powder, ½ pint chicken stock, juice of ½ lemon, 1 dessertspoon grated coconut, ½ bay leaf, 2 sprigs parsley, 1 teaspoon red currant jelly, pinch thyme.

Melt 3 oz. butter in frying pan. Add minced onion. Cook slowly for 2 minutes. Stir in flour and curry powder and cook for another couple of minutes. Add chicken stock, bay leaf, parsley and thyme. Simmer for ¼ hour, stirring occasionally. Steep coconut in ½ cup boiling water for 10 minutes. Add to curry sauce together with lemon juice and reed currant jelly. Cook for a further 5 minutes.

Cut the apple into chunks, skin bananas and cut into quarters. Gently fry in 1 oz. butter for about 4 minutes, turning from time to time.

Arrange fruit in oven-proof dish, pour curry sauce over it. Cook in slow oven (250° F.) for ½ hour. Serve with fluffy white rice.

Banana Honey

Ingredients: 6 firm bananas, ½ cup thin honey, ½ cup orange juice; 1 oz. butter, 1 dessertspoon toasted, ground hazelnuts.

Butter a shallow oven dish. Peel the bananas and arrange them in dish. Mix togther honey and orange juice. Pour this over the bananas. Cream butter, mix in ground nuts and place in spoonfuls over the bananas. Bake for 15 minutes in hot oven (450° F.), baste often.

Rhubarb Flummery

Ingredients: 1 lb. rhubarb, 4 oz. sugar, ½ pint water, 1 level tablespoon cornflour, 1 level dessertspoon gelatine, grated rind of 1 orange, shortbread fingers.

Lightly stew the rhubarb and sugar. Drain. Blend the cornflour with a little cold water then add to syrup. Return to heat and cook gently, stirring all the time, until mixture thickens. Soften the gelatine in 2 tablespoons cold water and add to the syrup mixture. Stir until it dissolves. Add grated rind of orange. When quite cold whisk well and fold in 2 tea cupfuls of the stewed rhubarb. Serve with shortbread fingers. As an addition this can be served with whipped cream.

Rhubarb Pudding

Ingredients: short crust pastry, ¾ lb. finely-chopped rhubarb, 4 oz. soft brown sugar, 2 oz. flour, grated rind ½ lemon, 3 tablespoons thick cream.

Line a plate with the pastry. Cover with the rhubarb which has been mixed with the cream, sugar and grated lemon rind. Bake in a moderately hot oven for 15 minutes, reduce heat and cook for a further 20 minutes or until the crust is crisp and the mixture firm.

Serve with whipped cream or custard sauce.

V

CITRUS FRUITS

Lemon Sponge

Ingredients: 1½ oz. sugar, ½ oz. gelatine, juice and grated rind 1 lemon, white of 1 egg, chopped nuts, whipped cream, ½ pint water.

Put the water, gelatine, lemon rind and juice into a pan and bring to the boil, stirring until dissolved. Simmer for 5 minutes. Strain and allow to cool.

Stiffly whisk the egg white and fold into the lemon mixture. Whisk until it is white and thick. Pour into a moistened mould. When set turn out and decorate with chopped nuts and whipped cream before serving.

Lemon Refresher

Ingredients: 1 tablespoonful lemon juice, 1 tablespoonful icing sugar, ½ pint milk, 2 table-spoonfuls cottage cheese, shortbread fingers.

Blend together the cottage cheese, lemon juice and icing sugar. Whip in the ½ pint milk. Serve with the shortbread fingers.

Hot Lemon Soufflé

Ingredients: 4 egg yolks, 4 egg whites beaten

stiff, grated rind and juice of 1 lemon, 6 oz.
caster sugar.

Beat the yolks until thick and lemon coloured. Beat in half the sugar gradually and add
lemon juice and rind. Beat the egg whites and
remaining sugar together until stiff. Fold into
the mixture. Bake for 40 minutes in a slow oven
—325° F. Serve hot with whipped chilled cream.

Lemon Meringue Pie

Ingredients: I ready-baked flan case, 1 tablespoonful cornflour, ¼ pint cold water, 6 oz.
caster sugar, grated rind and juice of 2 lemons,
yolk of 2 eggs, white of 2 eggs, pinch salt.

Place the cornflour and water in a pan and
mix well together. Add 4 oz. sugar and the
rind and juice of the lemons. Stir until boiling.
Simmer for 5 minutes. Cool, then add the egg
yolks. Pour into pastry case. Whip together the
egg whites and salt until stiff. Add half the remaining sugar and beat well. Fold in the remainder and pile on top of the lemon mixture.
Bake in a moderate oven until set and slightly
browned.

Lemon Froth

Ingredients: Juice and grated rind 1 lemon, ½
pint milk, 1 oz. cornflour, 2 oz. caster sugar, 1
egg yolk, 1 egg white.

Mix the cornflour to a smooth paste with a
tablespoonful of milk. Boil the remainder of

the milk. Stir in the cornflour, add the sugar.
Bring to the boil and cook for 3 minutes, stirring all the time. Cool slightly, beat in the egg
yolk. Add the lemon rind and juice and mix
well. Stiffly whisk the egg white and fold in.
Serve at once.

Orange Moules

Ingredients: 8 oz. shortcrust pastry made with
orange juice instead of water, 2 oz. butter, 2
oz. flour, 2 oz. sugar, pinch salt, 1 large egg
well beaten, 1 dessertspoon milk, 1 dessertspoon
orange juice, orange cheese.

Beat butter and sugar until creamy. Fold in
the egg and flour. Add the orange juice and
milk.

Line small tart cases with thinly rolled pastry.
Prick bottoms. Spread with orange cheese. Drop
a little cake mixture on top and level off. Trim
with two strips of pastry on top. Brush with
beaten egg or milk and bake in a moderate oven
for 20 minutes.

Orange Cheese

Ingredients: 2 eggs, 3 oz. sugar, grated rind 1
orange, 1 dessertspoonful orange juice, 1 teaspoon lemon juice, 1 oz. butter.

Mix together orange rind and sugar. Leave
for 10 minutes. Melt butter in a saucepan and
add the mixture to it. Add too the lemon and
orange juice and well beaten egg. Cook slowly

until thick. Store in clean jar if not required for immediate use.

In addition to being used in Orange Moules, Orange Cheese can be used hot or cold as a filling for cakes, tarts or flans. Children love it spread on toast or bread and butter.

Iced Orange Walnut Sponge

Ingredients: 3 eggs, 10 oz. caster sugar, 4 oz. butter, 4 dessertspoons fresh orange juice, 1 teaspoonful finely grated orange rind, pinch salt.

Cream 4 oz. sugar, and the eggs over hot water until they are warm. Remove from heat and beat thoroughly until thick and cold. Sieve flour and salt. Add orange rind. Fold in eggs and sugar. Add orange juice. Turn into a well-greased tin and bake in moderate oven for 50—60 minutes.

Remove from tin and leave to cool.

Make orange butter icing by creaming the 4 oz. butter thoroughly. Gradually add the 6 oz. caster sugar. Beat until fluffy then slowly stir in the 3 dessertspoonfuls orange juice.

Cut the sponge through twice and fill with butter icing. Sandwich together and cover top of cake also with icing. Decorate to taste with halved walnuts, pieces of angelica or a sprinkling of grated orange rind.

Orange Beignets

Ingredients: 4 oz. flour, 2 oz. butter, ¼ pint fresh

orange juice, 3 well-beaten eggs, 2 oz. sugar, rind of 1 orange, juice of 1 orange.

Put the butter and $\frac{1}{4}$ pint orange juice into a saucepan and bring up to boiling point. Remove from heat and mix in flour and $\frac{1}{2}$ oz. of the sugar quickly. Return to heat and cook, beating constantly. In a few minutes the mixture will leave the sides of the saucepan. Cool slightly and beat in the eggs and orange rind.

Fry small teaspoonful of the paste in deep fat or hot oil. Roll in sugar. Drain thoroughly on crumpled foil in a warm oven. The beignets should be crisp on the outside and smooth and creamy inside.

Serve with thick cream flavoured with orange juice.

Orange and Cheese Salad

Ingredients: 2 oranges, 4 oz. cottage cheese, $\frac{1}{2}$ cucumber, 1 tomato, small bunch watercress.

Peel the oranges and slice very finely. Wash the cucumber but do not peel. Slice very finely.

Arrange the cheese in the centre of large serving dish. Arrange the sliced orange and cucumber around the cheese. Garnish with tomato (cut in 8 wedges) and the watercress.

Orange Cream

Ingredients: For each serving—$\frac{1}{2}$ orange, 2 oz. thick whipped cream, 6 grapes, 1 glacé cherry.

Peel the orange then slice thinly. Arrange on a flat plate. Pile cream in centre and top with the grapes, or place them around the edge of the cream. Top with glacé cherry. Chill and serve.

Orange Surprise

Ingredients: ½ pint cream, 6 large oranges, 3 sponge cakes, 1 tablespoonful brandy or orange-flavoured liqueur, 2—3 oz. caster sugar.

Cut the tops off the oranges and scoop out the insides. Half fill the shells with sponge cake soaked in brandy and orange juice. Whip together the cream and the sugar. Pile this on top of the cake. Decorate with glacé cherries and leaves of angelica. Chill before serving.

Orange Delight

Ingredients: 3 large oranges, 1 packet orange-flavoured jelly, ½ pint cold custard.

Dissolve the jelly in ¾ pint hot water and leave until it starts to set. Prepare oranges by carefully removing the flesh from the segments. Whisk jelly until light and frothy. Fold in the prepared orange and cold custard. Turn into a wet mould. When set turn onto serving dish and decorate with orange slices and angelica or glacé cherries.

Stuffed Oranges

Ingredients: 2 large oranges, 2 eggs, $\frac{1}{2}$ oz. gelatine, 3 tablespoons one-minute oats, 2 tablespoons sugar, 2 oz. chocolate.

Cut a slice off the top of each orange and carefully remove the inside. Squeeze out the juice and mix it with the oats. Dissolve the gelatine in a little water. Heat juice, sugar and egg yolks until the mixture thickens. Add gelatine. Fold in the beaten egg whites and divide the mixture in two. Melt chocolate and add to half the mixture.

Place the oranges in cups and fill with the chocolate mixture. Allow to set. Top up with the remaining orange mixture. Allow to set then remove from cups and cut into quarters.

Orange Coconut Cream Pie

Ingredients: Juice and grated rind of 1 large orange, 1 teaspoon fresh lemon juice, 2 lightly beaten egg yolks, $\frac{1}{2}$ oz. butter, $\frac{3}{4}$ pint boiling water, 2 level dessertspoons cornflour, 6 oz. sugar, pinch salt, 3 dessertspoons shredded coconut, carton whipping cream, 1 baked pie shell.

Mix sugar, grated orange rind, salt and cornflour in the top of a double boiler. Stir in boiling water and cook, stirring all the time, until smooth and thick. Add 1 or 2 spoonfuls of the mixture to the beaten egg yolks and then mix all together in the top of the double boiler. Cook and stir again for a few minutes. Add the butter. Stir in and remove from heat. Mix in orange and lemon juice. Cool. Pour and spoon into the pie shell. Cover with the cream which has been whipped thick. Sprinkle with the coconut and serve.

Orange Pancakes

Ingredients: For the pancakes—4 oz. flour, 2 eggs, $\frac{1}{2}$ pint milk, pinch salt, 1 level dessertspoon icing sugar, 1 teaspoon brandy.

Sift flour, sugar and salt into bowl. Beat eggs and stir into the milk. Stir eggs and milk slowly into the flour mixture and beat until smooth. Finally add brandy. Allow to stand for $\frac{1}{2}$ hour. Use a small frying-pan and cook pancakes in oil or butter. As each pancake is cooked place flat on large plate or tin, sprinkle with a little brown sugar and keep warm over hot water until ready to serve.

For the sauce and garnish: 1 large orange (juice and rind), 2 oz. butter, 3 oz. icing sugar, liqueur glass of brandy or curaçao, 1 orange cut into segments (peel and all), 2 bananas, peeled and sliced.

Cream sugar and butter in small saucepan, add grated rind and juice and stir. Immediately before serving heat gently together with the brandy.

Place sliced bananas between pancakes. Pour

heated sauce over all and arrange orange segments and remaining banana slices around and
over the pancakes. Serve at once. Cut through
the pile in wedges after the manner of cake.

Orange and Cranberry Sauce

Ingredients: 1 large orange, 4 oz. cranberries, 3
oz. caster sugar.

Prick the cranberries with a knitting needle
or top of a pointed knife. Cut the orange in
half and squeeze the juice from one portion.
Place juice, sugar and cranberries in a small
saucepan and simmer gently until the cranberries are cooked. Do not allow to become
mushy. Remove the segments of orange from
the remaining half and stir into the sauce.
Serve while hot. Accompany with vanilla ice-
cream.

Orange Flip

Ingredients: ½ pint milk, strained juice 1 orange,
1 teaspoon caster sugar, 1 egg yolk.

Beat the egg yolk and sugar together until
creamy. Stir in the orange juice. Heat the milk
(do not boil) and gradually whisk this into the
orange mixture.
Serves 1 person.

Orange Cha Cha Cup

Ingredients: 4 medium-sized oranges, 8 dates,

1 tin red pimento, 1 grapefruit, honey and
grated nutmeg to taste. Mint leaves to garnish.

Peel oranges and grapefruit, divide into sections and halve each section, removing pips.
Arrange in a serving dish. Chop up dates and
add to bowl; drain tinned pimento, chop small
and add to rest of fruit. Grate a little nutmeg
over and warm the honey and pour over.

When serving, garnish each dish with fresh
mint leaves.

Baked Orange Creams

Ingredients: $\frac{1}{2}$ cup fresh orange juice, $\frac{1}{2}$ pint
scalded milk, 2 teaspoons grated orange rind,
2 eggs, separated, 6 oz. sugar, pinch salt, 1 level
tablespoon flour.

Beat egg whites stiff, add orange rind and salt
and beat a little more. Beat together egg yolks
and sugar, add orange juice, stir in flour. Mix
in the scalded milk. Fold in the beaten egg
whites. Butter individual souffle dishes and
spoon mixture into them. Place in a pan con-
taining $\frac{1}{2}$ in. hot water and place in moderate
oven (350° F.) for 30 minutes. Test with warm
skewer or knitting needle. Remove from oven
and chill.

Honey Orange Chantilly

Ingredients: 6 large oranges, 2 tablespoons thick
honey, 2 oz. butter, 2 tablespoons brown sugar,

water, ¼ pint thick cream, 1 teaspoon icing sugar, 4—6 drops vanilla flavouring.

Remove the centres from the oranges with an apple corer. Peel the fruit, using a very sharp knife and removing all the pith. Reserve any juice. Brush peeled oranges with melted butter. Roll them in brown sugar until coated all over. Stand in an ovenproof dish in 1 in. of water. Fill the hollowed centres with honey. Bake at 425° F. for 30 minutes. Serve hot. The juice in the dish acts as a sauce. Whip the cream, add icing sugar and vanilla flavouring and whip again until moderately stiff.

Oranges Scheherazade

Ingredients: 6 large oranges, ¼ lb. dates, 2 oz. blanched, shredded almonds, 2 tablespoons brandy, juice 2 oranges, 1 oz. caster sugar.

Peel the six oranges and remove white pith and pips. Slice them thinly into a large dish. Cover with sugar and dates which have been stoned and cut thinly. Pour over the brandy and strained orange juice. Leave for 12 hours. Turn into a deeper dish and top with the almonds.

Serve with unwhipped cream and sponge cake fingers.

VI

VEGETABLE FRUITS

Baked Pumpkin

Ingredients: 1 pumpkin, 2 oz. butter.

Cut the pumpkin into quarters and remove the seeds. Bake in a moderate oven for $1\frac{1}{2}$ hours. Serve with melted butter.

Pumpkin Fritters

Ingredients: 8 oz. cooked pumpkin, 4 oz. flour, 1 teaspoon baking powder, 2 eggs, $\frac{1}{4}$ teaspoon salt, 2 oz. caster sugar, 1 teaspoon cinnamon, 1 lemon, fat for frying.

Mix together thoroughly the pumpkin, flour, baking powder and salt. Add the beaten eggs and form into flat cakes about 3 inches in diameter and 1 in. deep. Fry until brown in deep smoking fat (lard or butter). Mix together the cinnamon and sugar and sprinkle over the cooked fritters. Serve with slices of lemon.

Pumpkin Syrup

Ingredients: 1 large pumpkin, sugar, cold water.

Wash the pumpkin and remove seeds and the soft centre. Cut into small cubes (skin and all); place in saucepan and just cover with water. Boil until soft then strain through a jelly bag. When all the juice has drained, put it in a pan and boil for 30 minutes. Measure the juice and add 1 cup of sugar to each cup of juice. Boil together until thick. Serve with pancakes or toast.

Pumpkin Pie

Ingredients: 6 oz. shortcrust pastry, 1 medium size pumpkin, 2 eggs, 6 oz. brown sugar, $\frac{1}{2}$ teaspoon ginger, juice and grated peel of 1 lemon, $\frac{1}{2}$ teaspoon cinnamon, vanilla, $\frac{1}{2}$ pint milk, $\frac{1}{4}$ pint cream.

Cover a large plate with rolled out pastry, prick all over and bake in moderate oven for 10 minutes.

Cut the pumpkin in half and remove the seeds. Bake in moderate oven until tender. Remove the flesh and sieve it. Mix with egg yolks, brown sugar, milk and flavourings. Whisk the egg whites and fold into pumpkin mixture. Arrange on pastry and bake in a hot oven for 15 minutes, then at reduced heat for a further 35 minutes.

Avocado Salad

Ingredients: 2 medium-size avocado pears, 2 cups grapefruit sections, $\frac{1}{2}$ dozen stuffed olives, french dressing.

Cut the pears into halves lengthwise and remove seeds. Scoop out the flesh leaving only sufficient to hold the shells in form. Cut the flesh removed into cubes and sprinkle with a little salt. Cut the grapefruit sections into pieces, slice olives into thin rounds. Mix all together then refill shells. Add a little French dressing and chill before serving.

Tomato and Orange Salad

Ingredients: 6 small tomatoes, 2 oranges, tomato ketchup, juice of ½ orange.

Peel the oranges and divide into segments. If the oranges are large ones the segments can be cut into halves. Peel and quarter the tomatoes and mix with orange segments. Dilute the tomato ketchup with the orange juice and mix all together.

Tomatoes with Eggs

Ingredients: 4 large tomatoes, 4 eggs, ½ oz. warmed butter, 2 oz. grated cheese, a little chopped parsley and fennel, fresh cream.

Slice off the stem end of the tomatoes, scoop out the pulp and seeds. Sprinkle a little salt and pepper inside each tomato and pour in a little warmed butter. Arrange the tomatoes on a well-buttered fireproof dish. Break an egg into each tomato, sprinkle with grated cheese, chopped parsley and fennel, dot with butter and replace the cut ends.

Bake in a moderate oven until tender, adding more butter if it is required. Serve with fresh cream.

Stuffed Tomato Salad

Ingredients: 4 tomatoes, 2 sticks celery, 2 rings pineapple, 2 oz. chopped walnuts, mayonnaise.

Cut the tops off the tomatoes, remove the pulp and seeds. Chop the celery, pineapple and mix all together with walnuts and mayonnaise. Fill the tomatoes with this mixture.

Stuffed Tomatoes

Ingredients: 4 large ripe tomatoes, 4 oz. cream cheese, 2 oz. chopped walnuts, chives, parsley.

Slice off the tops of the tomatoes and remove pips and flesh. Leave upside down to drain for 10 minutes. Sprinkle with salt and pepper. Mix together the cheese and walnuts and fill the tomato shells with the mixture. Garnish with chives and parsley.

Tomato Cob

Ingredients: 2 lb. tomatoes, 1 small onion, sugar, salt, pepper, ¼ pint double cream.

Mince together the tomatoes and onion and season to taste with the salt and pepper. A little sugar will be necessary only if the tomatoes are not fully ripe. Chill. Serve topped with the cream which has been well whipped.

Tomato Mayonnaise Dip with Prawns

Ingredients: 4 medium tomatoes, 16 medium-sized prawns, lemon mayonnaise.

Scoop out the rounded end of each tomato. Half fill with a spoonful of lemon mayonnaise. Arrange 4 prawns round the sides of each tomato, placing the waists of the prawns in the mayonnaise.

Tomato Tartlets with 3 Fillings

Any number of very small short pastry shells. Bake blind and crisp.

Filling 1.—TOMATO, CHOPPED TONGUE, AND MAYONNAISE.

Cut tongue in thickish slices and chop up. For every cup of chopped tongue, skin and chop up an equal amount of tomato, removing any hard core. Mix with thick mayonnaise to bind and add a few chopped capers if liked. Put a good spoonful into each tartlet. Garnish plate with spring onions and 2-in. sticks of chilled cucumber.

Filling 2.—TOMATO, CHOPPED HAM AND
    MAYONNAISE.

Cut slices of cold boiled ham rather thickly.
Cut slices into small pieces. Chop tomato pulp
scooped out of tomato shells. Flavour mayonnaise with a little made mustard. Mix sufficient of the flavoured mayonnaise with the
chopped ham and tomato to bind all together.
Pile into pastry shells.

Filling 3.—CHOPPED TOMATO, FLAKED WHITE
    FISH, CUCUMBER AND TARTARE SAUCE.

Flake any cooked cold white fish into a bowl,
removing skin and bones. Add chopped tomato
pulp, a little chopped cucumber and enough
tartare sauce to bind. Mix all together and pile
into tartlet shells.

VII

EXOTIC FRUIT

Pawpaw

Ingredients: 1 ripe pawpaw, $\frac{1}{2}$ lemon, sugar.

Cut the pawpaw in half and scoop out the
seeds. Cut the pawpaw in wedges. Cut the half
lemon in thick slices or wedges and serve with
pawpaw. Serve sugar separately.

Papaya (another name for Pawpaw)

Ingredients: ripe Papaya, lemon juice or lime
juice, sugar, ground ginger,

Cut the papaya in cubes, sprinkle over the
lemon or lime juice. Add ginger and sugar to
taste.

Japanese Persimmons

Take ripe fruit. Wash and dry the fruit and
serve it whole or in halves. It is served raw and
the soft inner flesh eaten with a spoon. This pulp
is extremely juicy.

Passion Fruit, or Granadilla

Ingredients: 12 passion fruit, 3 oz. sugar, $\frac{1}{2}$ pint
whipped cream.

Cut off the tops of the passion fruit and scoop out the fruit. Mix well with the sugar, add the cream and serve cold in individual glasses.

Passion Fruit Flan

Ingredients: 1 prepared flan case, 1 cup cooked passion fruit, 4 oz. sugar, ½ oz. gelatine, wedges of passion fruit (raw), whipped cream.

Dissolve the gelatine in a little water. Sieve the passion fruit, mix well with the sugar then stir into the gelatine. When nearly set pour into the pastry shell. Decorate with pieces of passion fruit and whipped cream.

Kumquats

Ingredients: 12—15 Kumquats, boiling water, 2 level dessertspoons golden syrup.

Soak the fruit in boiling water for 15 minutes. Remove, cut two gashes at the top end then arrange the fruit in a casserole. Run the golden syrup over the fruit. Bake in a cool oven 50—60 minutes.

Melon Salad

Ingredients: 1 ripe melon, ½ pint sherry, ¼ lb. sugar, 2 tablespoons Sloe Gin, or Cherry Brandy, pinch salt.

Cut the melon into ¾ in. cubes. Remove the seeds. Mix well together the sherry, Sloe Gin, sugar and pinch of salt. When the sugar has completely melted pour this mixture over the cubes of melon. Place in refrigerator for 1 hour to chill. Serve in individual glasses on lettuce leaves.

Melon Cocktail

Ingredients: 1 slice water melon, 1 slice cantaloupe melon, juice 1 lemon, juice 1 orange, 3 tablespoons chopped mint, 2 oz. sugar.

Boil the sugar with $\frac{1}{4}$ pint water for 5 minutes. Pour over the mint. Mix together the orange and lemon juice. From the melon slices cut out as many small balls or chunks as possible. Chill well and add to the drink just before serving.

Brandy Cantaloupe

Ingredients: 1 cantaloupe melon, juice 1 lemon, 4 oz. icing sugar, 1 wineglass brandy, glacé cherries, whipped cream.

Peel the melon, remove the seeds and chop the flesh into cubes. Mix together the brandy, icing sugar and lemon juice and pour over these cubes. Cover tightly and place in the refrigerator or other cool place for about 2 hours. Serve in individual glasses, topped with whipped cream and garnished with a glacé cherry.

Melon with Pineapple

Ingredients: 1 medium size ripe melon, 1 small

pineapple, 1 tablespoon chopped mint, 4 oz. sugar, 6 black grapes.

Peel the pineapple and cut into small cubes. Cover with sugar. Wash the melon then slice in half and remove the seeds. Fill each half with pineapple. Place in refrigerator or cool place for 1 hour. Immediately before serving sprinkle with mint and garnish with grapes.

Fig Squares

Ingredients: 8 oz. figs, ½ pint water, 6 oz. caster sugar, 1 teaspoon lemon juice, 6 oz. self-raising flour, ½ level teaspoon salt, 6 oz. cooking fat, 6 oz. rolled oats.

Sieve together the flour, salt and 4 oz. caster sugar. Rub in the cooking fat until the mixture resembles breadcrumbs. Add the rolled oats and mix well.

Divide the mixture in half. Press one half in the bottom of a well greased tin (7 in. x 11 in. is the ideal size).

Chop the figs and cook them over a low heat with the water and 2 oz. caster sugar. Stir frequently. Add the lemon juice. Place the mixture in the tin and spread evenly. Cover with remaining oat mixture and press down firmly.

Bake on the middle shelf of a moderate oven (400° F.) for 15—20 minutes. When almost cool cut into 12—14 squares.

Quince and Apple Pancakes

Ingredients: 1 pint pancake batter, 2 lb. cooking apples, 1 quince, 3 oz. caster sugar, 2 tablespoons water. Few slices lemon.

Peel, core and slice apples and quince. Stew gently with sugar and water until tender. Keep warm while the pancake batter is being cooked.

Make pancakes in normal way, brown on both sides and turn onto sugared paper. Add a dessertspoonful of apple and quince filling, then roll up and keep warm while frying remaining pancakes, or serve immediately. Decorate with lemon quarters.

Quince and Apple Sauce

Ingredients: 1 quince, 3 cooking apples, ½ pint cider, 4 oz. sugar, 1 oz. butter.

Peel, core and chop the fruit. Put into a saucepan with the cider and bring up to boiling point. Simmer until fruit is tender. Stir frequently using a wooden spoon. If the pulp is too thin strain off a little of the liquid. Add the sugar and continue to cook gently until this is melted. Stir in the butter. Serve hot with roast pork or goose. Serve cold with shortbread fingers.

Quince Fondants

Ingredients: Quinces, sugar.

Wash the quinces, remove their core and chop into pieces. Steam them until they are tender then pass through a sieve. Place the purée with an equal weight of sugar, in a preserving pan and boil gently. Stir until it thickens and comes away from the sides of the pan. Beat well, then pour into shallow tins and leave in a cool oven to harden. Cut in 1-inch squares, wrap in greaseproof paper and store in an airtight tin.

Stuffed Quinces

Ingredients: 6 quinces, ¼ lb. minced cooked chicken, salt to taste, 2 dessertspoons honey, 1 oz. butter.

Wash and core the quinces, cover with boiling water and gently cook for 20 minutes. Place in a shallow fireproof dish, after draining them and filling with the minced chicken which has been seasoned to taste. Dot with butter and bake in a moderate oven for 50—60 minutes.

Stuffed Pineapple

Ingredients: 1 large pineapple, 1 large cupful fruit salad, 2 tablespoons sherry (optional), whipped cream.

Slice off the top of the pineapple and with a sharp knife remove the flesh from the centre. Mix this with the fruit salad and marinade in the sherry, leave for 1 hour. Return the fruit to the pineapple alternating layers of fruit with layers of whipped cream. Top with a swirl of cream.

Pineapple Balls

Ingredients: 1 cupful finely chopped pineapple, caster sugar, 2 eggs, 4 oz. flour, pinch salt, ¼ pint milk, fat for deep frying.

Make a thick batter with the flour, eggs, salt and milk. When smooth add the pineapple and mix well. When the fat is smoking hot drop in the mixture, a dessertspoonful at a time. Fry until golden brown, drain well, roll in caster sugar.

Serve at once.

Pineapple Fritters

Ingredients: 1 pineapple, 2 oz. sugar, 4 oz. flour, ¼ pint milk, ¼ teaspoon salt, 1 egg.

Sieve together the flour and salt. Add the beaten egg and one third of the milk. Mix until smooth, add the rest of the milk and leave to stand for 1 hour.

Peel the pineapple and cut in ½-in. rings. Sprinkle with sugar. Dip each piece into the batter then fry in very hot fat until golden brown outside. Dust with sugar before serving.

Flaked Pineapple

Ingredients: 1 pineapple, 4 oz. sugar, ½ pint cream.

Peel and grate the pineapple, stir in the sugar and mix until the sugar is dissolved. Place in individual serving dishes. Serve with the cream which has been whipped until fairly thick.

Pineapple Salad

Ingredients: 2 slices of cooked ham cut fairly thick, 2 rings of pineapple, 3 oz. cottage cheese, 1 lettuce.

Dice the ham and pineapple and mix together. Line a plate with washed lettuce leaves. Pile the cottage cheese in the centre, arrange the ham and pineapple all round.

Pineapple Flip

Ingredients: 1 thick slice pineapple, ¼ pint pineapple juice, ½ pint milk, 1 egg, 3 dessertspoons caster sugar, 1 teaspoon Aromatic Bitters, cherries to garnish.

Whisk together the milk, egg yolk and 1 dessertspoon sugar. Blend in the pineapple juice and bitters.

Whisk the egg white to a stiff froth with remaining sugar and fold into mixture. Pour into two long glasses and serve with straws threaded with wedges of pineapple and cherries.

VIII

FRUIT SALADS AND MIXED FRUIT DISHES

Assorted Fruit Salad

Ingredients: Any available assorted fruits, ½ pint water, 4 oz. sugar, dessertspoon lemon juice, colouring if desired.

Clean and prepare the fruit. Large fruits can be halved or sliced or diced. Place in a large serving dish and mix well.

Boil togther the sugar and water until they form a syrup. Remove from heat. Add lemon juice and colouring. Pour this over the mixed fruit. Allow to cool and chill before serving.

Fruit and Nut Salad

Ingredients: 1 cupful grapes, 1 cupful chopped Brazil nuts, ½ cup shredded apple, ½ cup shredded pineapple, 1 dessertspoon lemon juice or orange juice, whipped cream.

Skin the grapes and cut them in half lengthwise. Mix well with the other fruit and nuts. Sprinkle with lemon juice. arrange on lettuce leaves in individual portions. Serve the cream separately.

Pavlova Fruit Salad

Ingredients: Assorted fruit, ¼ pint sugar syrup,

4 egg whites, 8 oz. caster sugar, vanilla pod,
¼ pint double cream, 4 oz. ice-cream, ½ lb.
raspberries.

Marinade the prepared fruit in the sugar
syrup for at least 1 hour. Beat the egg whites
very stiff, fold in the sugar and flavour with
vanilla. Line the bottom and sides of a tart
tin with greaseproof paper and put the meringue mixture into this making a depression in
the centre. Bake in a slow oven for 2 hours.
Leave to cool then turn out of the tin onto a
large plate. Drain the fruit and pile into centre
of meringue. When ready to serve top with ice-
cream, whipped cream and raspberries.

Fruit Purée

Ingredients: Assorted fruit, whipped cream, 2
oz. chopped nuts.

Cook all the fruit together until it is soft.
Press it through a sieve and leave to cool.
Serve in cups with cream and chopped nuts as a
garnish.

Raw Fruit Soup

Ingredients: Assorted ripe fruit, 4 oz. sugar, ¼
pint water, dessertspoon lemon juice; dessertspoon orange juice.
Prepare the fruit, peeling and coring when
necessary. Chop and rub through sieve. Add
orange or lemon juice, or both, to flavour. Make

a syrup with the sugar and water and while still hot pour over the fruit.

Compôte of Fruit

Ingredients: 2 lb. assorted fruit, 6 oz. sugar, ½ pint water, 1 dessertspoon lemon juice.

Bring the sugar and water to boiling point. Wash and prepare the fruit and add to the syrup. Cook gently until the fruit is soft. Do not overheat. Before serving add the lemon juice. This dish can be eaten hot or cold.

Mixed Fruit Jelly

Ingredients: 6 oz. fresh red currants, 6 oz. fresh blackcurrants; 6 oz. strawberries, 6 oz. black cherries, ½ pint cider or white wine, ¼ pint water, 1 oz. gelatine, ½ lb. caster sugar, whipped cream.

Top and tail the currants, hull the strawberries and stone the grapes. Stew the currants with the sugar and water and then sieve them. Mix the gelatine with a little of the wine then pour the hot purée over it. Add the rest of the fruit and the wine and pour into a mould to set.

Serve with the whipped cream.

Fruit Chiffon Pie

Ingredients: 1 prepared pie crust, 1 banana,

1 tablespoon lemon juice, 3 tablespoons orange juice, 1 cup crushed pineapple, ¼ pint thick cream, 6 oz. sugar, 1 tablespoon gelatine.

Slice the banana, soak in the fruit juices. Add the pineapple. Dissolve the gelatine in a little cold water. Add the fruit and sufficient hot water to make up to 1 pint. Leave to set. When almost set, fold in the cream which has been well whipped. Turn into the baked pie crust and place in refrigerator for 30 minutes to chill.

Fruit Syrup

Ingredients: ½ pint fruit juice, 2 oz. sugar, ¼ pint whipped cream; 1 dessertspoon powdered gelatine.

Blend the gelatine with a little of the fruit juice. Bring the remainder of the juice to the boil and pour over. Return to heat and stir until gelatine has dissolved. Cool, then beat until thick and light. Keep very cold when whipping, either stand the basin in cold water or in a larger container and surround with crushed ice. Fold in the whipped cream.

Steamed Fresh Fruit Pudding

The fruit used to make this can change with the varying seasons. It tastes equally good when filled with any of the following: rhubarb, gooseberries, raspberries and red currants, blackcurrants, plums, damsons, blackberries and apples.

Ingredients: 12 oz. plain flour, 3 oz. margarine, 3 oz. butter, 1 teaspoon baking powder, pinch salt, 2 lb. suitable fruit, 2 tablespoons sugar (or more for very sour fruit), grated rind $\frac{1}{2}$ lemon.

Prepare the fruit, large hard fruit should be diced or sliced.

Sift the flour, salt and baking powder together, chop the butter and margarine and rub into the flour. Stir well with a knife and gradually add 3—4 tablespoons cold water to form a firm dough.

Reserve $\frac{1}{4}$ paste for the lid, roll out remainder and line a 2 pint basin with it. Grease the basin well first. Put in half the prepared fruit, sprinkle with the sugar and lemon rind, add the remainder of the fruit and a little cold water. Roll out the rest of the pastry to the size of the top of the basin. Moisten the edges and join carefully to the edges of the pastry in the basin. Tie two folds of tin-foil over the top and steam for $2\frac{1}{2}$—3 hours. Best method of doing this is in a saucepan that has a tight-fitting lid. The boiling water in the saucepan should reach to about half the depth of the basin and should be kept at this level by occasionally adding more boiling water.

When cooked, lift basin out and remove tin foil. Allow some of the steam to escape before turning onto a warmed dish or plate.

Serve with custard sauce or with real cream.

Spring Compôte of Fruits

Ingredients: ½ lb. black and white grapes, 1 large orange, 2 fresh peaches, 3 large plums, 1 small pineapple, 2 pears, 4 oz. sugar, juice 1 lemon, 3 tablespoons water.

Boil the sugar and water together for 5 minutes to make a syrup. Add lemon juice and any juice that results from preparing the fruit.

To prepare the fruit, peel orange and cut carefully in thin slices, removing any pips. Skin peaches and cut in halves. Wash plums and cut in halves, removing stones. Peel, core and quarter pears. Remove rind from pineapple, cut in thick slices and then dice. Mix all in serving bowl then pour over the hot syrup and leave to cool. When quite cold garnish with the grapes which should be washed, sliced in half and de-pipped.

Serve with a bowl of sweetened whipped cream to which a few drops of Kirsch has been added before beating.

Quick Fruit Salad

Ingredients: 1 pear, 1 orange, 1 apple, few grapes or any other soft fruit.

Prepare the fruit and slice, dice or halve as necessary. Arrange in individual serving dishes.

Serve with top-of-the-milk, whipped cream, or vanilla ice-cream.

INDEX